LEAN for the Nonprofit

WHAT YOU DON'T KNOW CAN COST YOU

by

PADDY O'BRIEN

MPA, Lean Certified, GBLSS, OPMA

INKWATER PRESS

PORTLAND • OREGON
INKWATERPRESS.COM

For more information on this book scan this QR Code

Cover and interior design by Masha Shubin

Publisher: Inkwater Press | www.inkwaterpress.com

ISBN-13 978-1-62901-411-1 | ISBN-10 1-62901-411-7

Printed in the U.S.A.

3 5 7 9 10 8 6 4 2

Table of Contents

Current Facts About Nonprofits

How Many? Approximately 1.41 million nonprofits were registered with the Internal Revenue Service (IRS) in 2013, an increase of 2.8 percent from 2003.

Size. Even after excluding organizations with gross receipts below the $50,000 filing threshold, *small* organizations composed the majority of public charities in 2013.

Contribution to Economy. The nonprofit sector contributed an estimated *$905.9 billion* to the US economy in 2013, composing 5.4 percent of the country's gross domestic product (GDP).

A Quarter of Our Citizens Volunteer. Fully 25.3 percent of US adults volunteered with an organization in 2014, contributing an estimated 8.7 billion hours ... *valued at $179.2 billion.*

Finances. Fully 58.6 percent of nonprofit organizations reporting to the IRS in 2013 were public charities .... Assets held by public charities accounted for more than three-fifths of the sector's total (*$3.22 trillion*).

Source: The Urban Institute, October 2015

Preface

Why do I write this primer? Because donors do not want their money to go to waste, clients want to get the best possible services, and staff and volunteers deserve a different kind of support.

For those of you who haven't heard of Lean,* it is not an acronym. It is a manufacturing method popularized by Toyota. Its essence is to streamline workflows so they are without any excess or costly steps. Today it has been adopted by industries such as healthcare, service-type businesses, and local governments. In fact, there is evidence of Lean all around you: when you go to get your morning coffee and they take your order and then repeat that order three different times, that is Lean's concept of "quality at the source." When you fly on that airline and they don't offer meals or extra frills, that is so they can pass on cost savings to you. That is Lean too. Yes, there are some nonprofits who have tried Lean, but as a whole, the nonprofit world, unlike healthcare, has yet to be informed of its value.

In a time of scarce resources and competing for donors, nonprofit organizations should not have to cut programs in order to balance their budgets. Lean provides an alternative. Learn how to find hidden costs in your operations ... and do something else with that money.

* Lean is term first coined by John F. Krafcik, "Triumph in the Lean Production System," Sloan Management Review, 1988. It is used to distinguish itself from mass production.

Introduction

Ever since the recession of 2008, competition for dollars is more intense than ever. Any nonprofit that embeds sound business practices into meeting their mission will have the edge.

The challenges unique to nonprofit organizations are formidable. Most of their financial support relies on donations, and this puts them at the mercy of the economy. And most of their work is carried out by small staffs and volunteers, who come with great passion but have little management acumen. Using Lean methods helps find hidden unnecessary costs; the money spent on those costs can be reallocated. Also, the Lean methodology uses the organization's staff to participate on improvement teams. What the teams learn about management principles and tools is invaluable.

Lean in Action—Nonprofit

Not very many people know this, but in the zoo business, it is essential to refresh and build new exhibits in order to "stay in business." In late 2007, when the Monroe Zoo's budget was robust, there was enough money to build a new koala exhibit. The staff knew this would be a boon to the community. Then the recession of 2008 hit. The zoo's budget was at the mercy of the economy, and as a consequence, the "new" exhibit line item was cut from the budget.

The tenacious zoo staff sought an alternative. The newspaper reported that the local hospital was using Lean to streamline their admissions process. The zoo staff visited the hospital team and ultimately received training in Lean techniques.

A zoo improvement team consisting of selected staff was formed to do a workshop. In Lean this is called a Rapid Process Improvement (RPI) workshop. It's the forum for the improvement work to be done. The improvement team followed the Lean method of removing all unnecessary (waste) steps from their operations processes. Every step zoo staff performed had the costs of labor, time, and materials attached to it. In addition to the unnecessary steps, there were other hidden costs caused by bottlenecks (work stoppage costs money). The zoo improvement team set out to find the root causes of the bottlenecks (otherwise they would only be providing a Band-Aid to the problem).

They focused on the operations processes that support the programs of the zoo. These operations were:

- Ticket sales
- Cleaning of exhibits
- Paying the employees
- Maintaining the grounds
- Monitoring the health of the animals
- Etcetera

The team started working on the payroll process. This was selected because employees were complaining about errors on their pay stubs. The team examined the process from the time an employee submitted a time sheet until he/she received a paycheck. The team collected baseline data to determine the cycle time of processing the paycheck and developed a checklist of the number and kind of pay stub mistakes. They developed a picture (a flowchart) of the payroll process.

Zoo Payroll Process

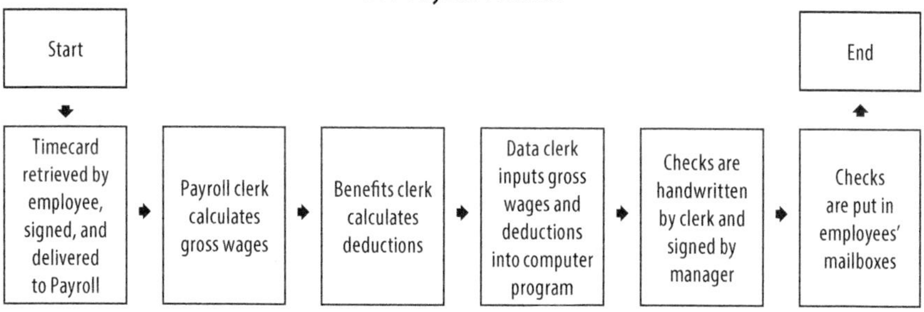

Using a flowchart with added detailed steps, they checked each step for its value. They marked each step as "value," "waste," or "necessary." ("Necessary" can be because a law requires it.)

Step by Step Analysis

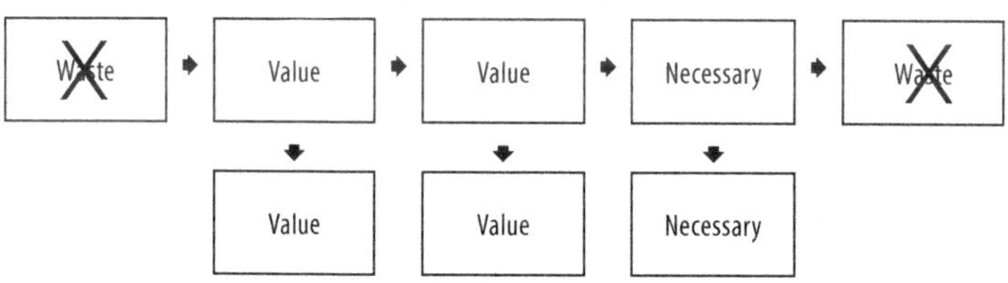

Examples of waste were those steps no longer needed but still used, those that were duplications of steps that had already been completed, and those that were so obviously waste, such as checkers checking the checkers. They simply removed these steps and tallied their costs.

Then the team tackled those obstacles that, like bottlenecks, were preventing a smooth flow of the work. They selected the ticketing process as their focus. To understand this process, they first observed it in action. They stood near the ticket booths and entry gates. This is what they saw: on heavy visiting days like Saturdays and Sundays, there were long lines to get tickets. Many visitors left before they got to the ticket window, and others waited but appeared very unhappy. After observing, they completed their root cause analysis of the long lines. They made the following improvements: they assigned different kinds of ticket sales to different windows. One was made into an "express window" for zoo members, another was designated for those buying tickets for future dates, and then the remaining two were used for daily visitors. But their improvements didn't end there. They automated the tickets sales so that when a ticket sale was made, it went into a computer that allowed people to enter through a counter gate without waiting to hand in a ticket.

Their work continued. Inside the gate, there were different flow problems. Feedback from a visitors' survey was utilized. Answers from the parents who brought children to the zoo were loud and clear. They complained that the layout of the zoo scattered the kid-centric exhibits all over the grounds. The long walks for children were very tiring and parents questioned whether they would visit the zoo again.

This is what the team did: after looking at a blueprint for the grounds and calculating the cost of time spent to get to an exhibit, the improvement team simply decided to reconfigure the location of the exhibits. All the kid-centric exhibits were moved closer together and nearer to the main gate.

When the team's research and recommendations were completed, they met with zoo management. This is what they reported. Not only did they make improvements in the old way of running the zoo, but they acquired new skills they could take back to their jobs: how to collect data, how to develop a flowchart, how to know what works and what doesn't, and how important the visitor is to the success of the zoo. They reported what they did: they streamlined the tasks, took out duplicative steps, made things run smoothly without stalling, and kept all operations focused on what the visitor to the zoo wanted.

The end result: money that was no longer spent on waste was

recouped. And that money was used to build the koala exhibit. But the big surprise was an unexpected windfall: as the popularity of the koala exhibit grew, so did their overall revenue!

CHAPTER 1

What is Lean?

Where do we start?

We start with a simple definition. Lean is a management method that focuses on workflows, or what we call processes. A process is a series of steps that flow sequentially; each process has a customer at the completion of the process who receives the product or service. Processes do not stand alone. They are part of a bigger picture. When an organization develops a strategic plan it develops processes to do the work that implements the strategies.

The big picture can be perceived through the lens of an organization chart ...

... or through a chart that shows your organization as a series of interconnected processes.

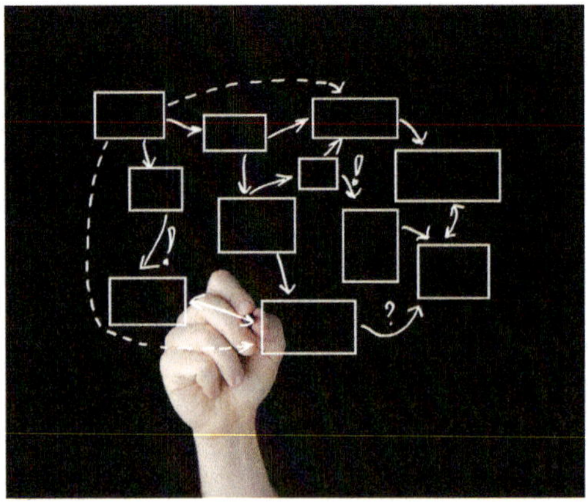

When a customer (or a citizen or a student or a patient) of your process views your organization, they do not see a hierarchical, organization chart of managers and subordinates, they see the workflows, the processes. Those processes deliver to the customers what they require. In Lean, it is the customer who determines whether the processes are operating as they should. By understanding what the customer requires and then developing a measure to see if the requirement is met by your processes, your organization will know immediately whether the process needs improvement.

Customer Tree

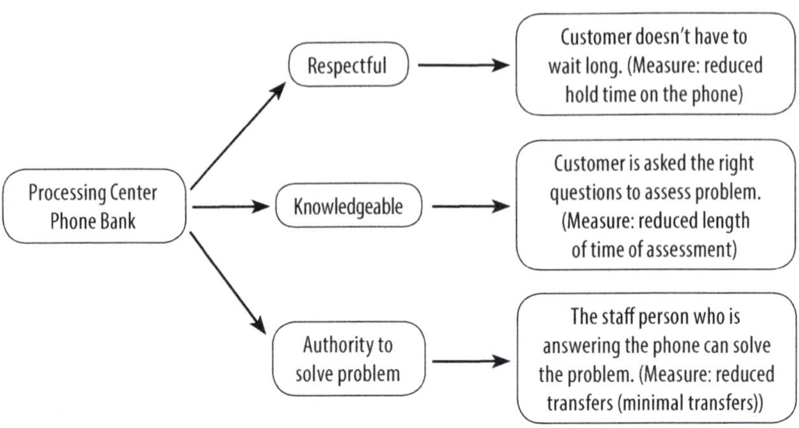

In Lean, improving processes is done in a prescribed way. For example, when an error was discovered in a Toyota factory, the work stopped briefly to see if the problem could be solved. If a customer wanted a blue car but a white car was delivered instead, the factory floor workers (who actually did the work) got together to figure out what went wrong in the process. This huddle action became known as a *kaizen* event. The Japanese developed the concept of *kaizen* because it helped the entire organization to be more efficient. Note *kaizen*'s distinctive characteristics: workers are asked to give their input, the root cause of a problem is discovered, and the problem is solved quickly and simply. For this car color problem, the workers came up with a simple Lean tool: stop the mistake at the source. In this case, they recommended putting an error-proofing tool in place at the paint station.

Modeling what happens on the factory floor, *kaizen* events are held in many organizations and are also known as Rapid Process Improvement (RPI) workshops.

This is a structured workshop made up of a small team of staff, managers, and customers who learn to apply Lean improvement concepts to workflow problems. The team is guided by a trained facilitator and a written charter and meets for a compressed period of time that lasts from two to five days, depending on the complexity of the problem. The team gathers data, conducts experiments, and makes recommendations for improvements in a final presentation to an executive team.

Lean in Action—Healthcare

While visiting one of Seattle's hospitals (hospitals in this area were influenced by Boeing, also located there; Boeing was one of the first adopters of Lean in the US), in particular, one that has pioneered Lean in healthcare, I was invited to the improvement team's final report to management at the completion of a four-day Rapid

Process Improvement workshop. The workshop had focused on the preparation of surgical trays. What was the problem? Surgeons (the customer) were complaining that the trays were often without needed surgical tools.

The improvement team (made up of workers such as nurses) collected data and discovered the tray preparation process was fraught with errors.

Before each surgery, surgical trays with carefully laid out instruments are prepared for the doctor. Each surgeon has his/her own special list (based on the type of operation) that is given to the nurse who prepares the trays. However, the list is always given to the nurse *at the last minute*. There is little time to prepare the trays and mistakes are made.

Invariably, during the surgery the surgeon calls for a tool that is not on the tray. Whoops! The nurse scurries out of the operating room to hunt down the tool. Time is lost in the surgery, the patient could be at risk, and the surgeon is not happy.

Now the improved process: the improvement team surveyed the surgeons and got all of them to agree to a core set of tools (no special brand names and such) that could be put on every tray. This commonality allowed trays to be set up well before the surgeries. Then, at the last minute, each surgeon's *special list* of tools could be added. This improvement was literally a "lifesaver."

CHAPTER 2

Show me how it works!

First, the concepts, then the training, and then see an RPI at work! When a problem occurs, an organization can react in one of two ways. Let me share an example with you: I have seen a child protective service organization react to a negative news article by immediately changing all of their procedures. This is a different reaction than what would happen in a Lean organization. In this case, the staff would collect data about what caused the incident that was reported and determine whether this happened one time or many times. If it happened many times, this would be attributed to a system problem rather than the occasional human error. An RPI workshop would be convened. The workshop would get at the root cause of the problem), and the data collected during the workshop would support the appropriate recommendations for changes.

Asked by the executive director: "If I was to call for an improvement workshop in my organization, what happens in the office environment?"

Well, the news would spread quickly throughout the staff and some may wonder if the problem at hand involves them. So it is very important that the executive team stop any rumors by communicating to all staff about the upcoming workshop: the dates, subject, and staff members on the team. Usually, this announcement takes place a month before the actual workshop begins. There will be preliminary activity that all will see as the workshop facilitator begins collecting baseline data and interviewing some staff in order to develop initial flowcharts. This involves short interruptions of some daily work but doesn't last long. What is important here is to communicate with the entire staff about what is happening in preparation for the workshop.

The workshop will, ideally, be taking place near the workplace itself, off the main area, or close by, in a conference room that will be used as a team room. For the next several days, the workshop team and those staff not on the team will experience different things. For the staff in the workplace, they will see the one or more members of the workshop team go in and out of the conference room to perform workshop activities. Some activities will just be observations; some will involve analyses of files. The team is advised to be respectful of each worker's time and that if they need to talk to a worker, to schedule an appointment.

Again, communication with all the staff is very important. Outside the team room, a flip-chart posts the workshop's completed activities at the end of each day. Anyone can stop by and read it to know what is going on.

Now, inside the team room, the team is having a very different experience. Although they were sent a welcome memo and knew vaguely of what to expect, there is usually surprise as to the great amount of work to be done in just a few short days, and they may ask themselves, "Can we do this?"

Sample Welcome Memo

From: Your Facilitator
To: The New Team Members
Date: 12/03/16
Subject: Welcome to the RPI Workshop!

Hello everyone,

You have been selected to sit on the Rapid Process Improvement

Team that will address improvement in the process that allocates federal award monies to the American Agencies on Aging (AAAs).

The workshop will take place on January 8, 9, and 10. The location will be somewhere in the DHS building, and I'll let you know exactly where as we get closer to the date.

For those of you who do not know about the RPI, it is an intense two- or five-day workshop where we come together as a team. We contribute our best thinking to make improvements on processes that are not working as well. During the workshop, I will be teaching you Lean Thinking methods that will help you think about streamlining the current processes. We will be collecting data, analyzing the cause of problems, and redesigning procedures, methods, or forms.

Lee is the contact lead for this workshop. Mike B. will be our 'barrier-buster' and Cathy C. is our workshop sponsor.

There is some prep work that needs to be done before the workshop begins. We will need to start collecting our baseline.

The facilitator assures the team that they indeed are up to the task! It is up to the trained facilitator to turn these separate individuals into a team, to make sure they are given the proper tools, and to guide them through the workshop agenda to meet the intended goals of the RPI, removing waste and improving the flow of the work. To emphasize these goals, the facilitator reminds the team "that a Lean process is simply using only the minimal amount of resources to get the job done."

Anything other than "what is essential" is considered waste. We saw that with the zoo example when the improvement team removed unnecessary and duplicative steps from the payroll process.

> In the 1930s, Kiichiro Toyoda, the founder of Toyota, coined a term "just-in-time." He explained how each station of the assembly process should only manufacture "what is required, when it is required, and in the exact quantity required."

The other Lean goal is to move the goods or services through the process so that they reach the customer on time and without errors. An example for *on time* is when the zoo case study showed the visitors trying to get through the ticket process and having to wait too long. And *errors* were made in the hospital example: the surgical trays were prepared in a way that caused key instruments to be left out.

To back up just a bit, it is important to know that necessary training for the team cannot use up the days set aside for the actual workshop. So prior to the first day of the workshop, the team will spend time learning *the basic goals of Lean* and the path to achieve them. In addition to this, they are taught the importance of data in decision-making. The schematic you see here was developed with the ordinary worker in mind; all tools are easy to learn.

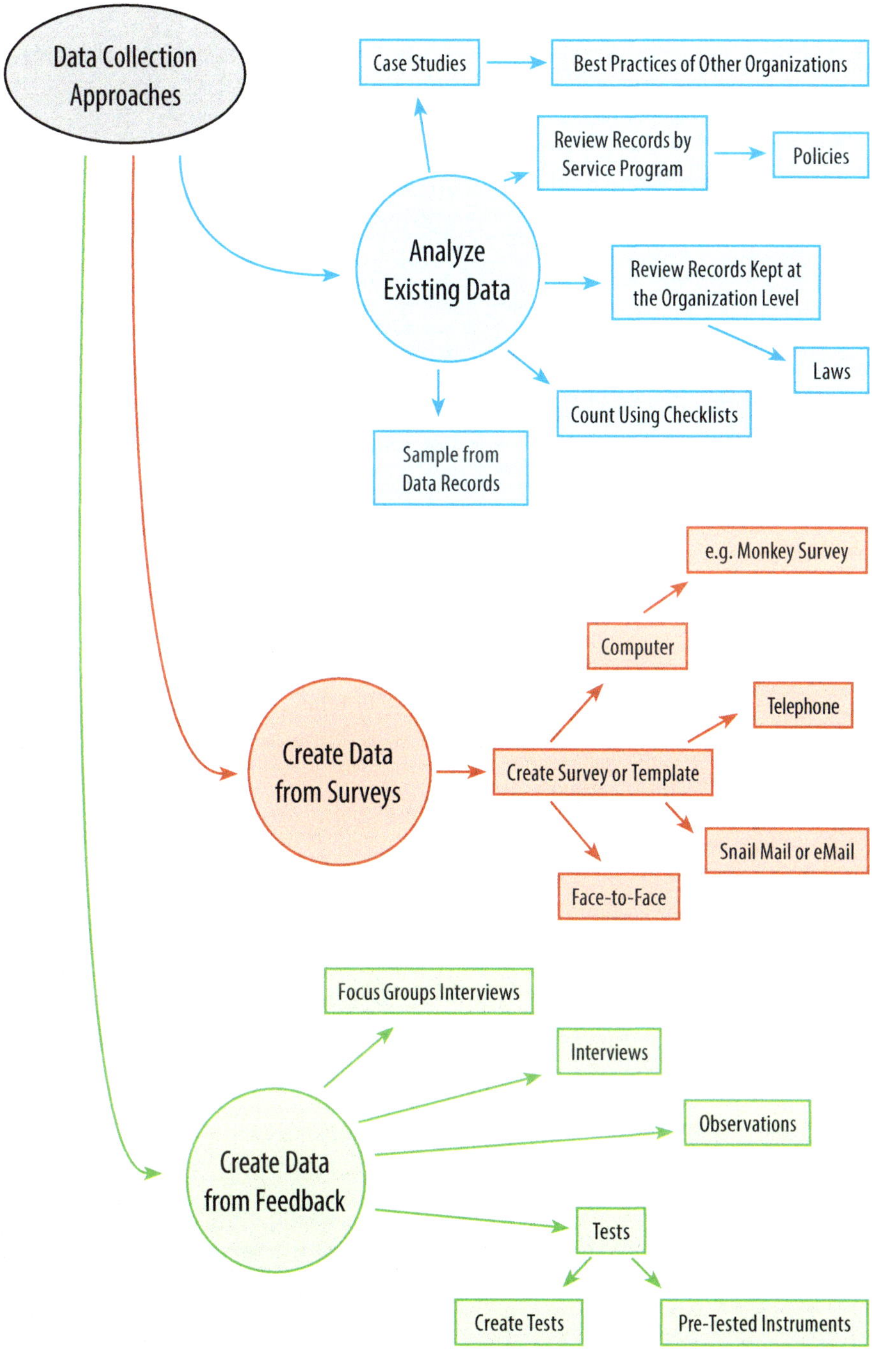
Data Collection Approaches
Case Studies
Best Practices of Other Organizations
Review Records by Service Program
Policies
Analyze Existing Data
Review Records Kept at the Organization Level
Laws
Count Using Checklists
Sample from Data Records
e.g. Monkey Survey
Computer
Telephone
Create Data from Surveys
Create Survey or Template
Snail Mail or eMail
Face-to-Face
Focus Groups Interviews
Interviews
Observations
Create Data from Feedback
Tests
Create Tests
Pre-Tested Instruments

For the rest of the training, the facilitator knows learning Lean goals can be very abstract at first. But the workshop pace doesn't have time for "abstract." So metaphors are used to quicken the process of ingraining Lean theory into the team's thinking.

The metaphor teaching begins with what a customer expects: the first expectation is about timeliness. Whatever is ordered as a product, or requested as a service, must be delivered on time. Late delivery can be attributed to unnecessary steps being performed in the process, and this means more resources are being used than is needed to get the job done. Pruning a tree can be likened to taking the waste out of a process bogged down by unnecessary and, therefore, wasteful steps.

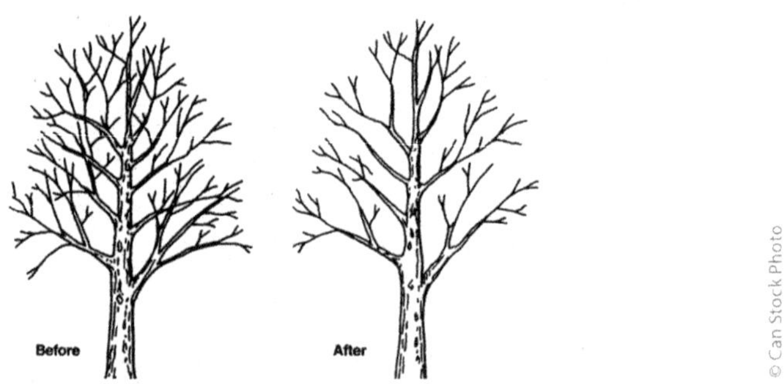

Consider, the orchardist is supposed to keep the trees healthy. One of the routine assessments is to see if a tree needs pruning and when that should be done. If the tree is not periodically thinned out, the water and nutrients needed to grow the tree are sparsely and wastefully distributed throughout the trunk and the branches. In addition, fuller and fuller branches start getting entangled, and this eventually chokes new growth!

Again, starting with the customer, timeliness is critical. If the flow of the process is not smooth, that is, it has a lot of delays, the delivery will be late. The concept of "flow" can also be abstract. It helps to think about it in the opposite way, or "the lack of flow." How about a freeway at rush hour? The traffic *flow* has many delays and the driver will arrive late.

Now think of what you would do to improve this lack of flow? Consider this: creating a smooth workflow without any stops and gos is like driving through a roundabout.

The roundabout is a replacement for the traffic intersection with the four-way stop.

It is a wonderful depiction of a Lean continuous flow. Look at the characteristics that make it so: there are no stop signs, only yield signs. Drivers already in the circle are affected by yield signs, and this changes the pace of traffic. A new driver entering the circle doesn't stop, only slows down to look for an opening before merging into the flow of traffic. If the entering driver doesn't speed up quickly to drive at the speed required, cars back up and valuable time is lost.

In summary, when you need to remember what Lean is, think of pruning a tree or driving through a roundabout!

A Real Life Case Study: Rapid Process Improvement

Process: applying for admission into a health plan

This case study is about the eligibility process of the health plan insurance system in our state. This system is responsible for providing health insurance to people who normally can't afford it. This cascading schematic includes a business system and its processes.

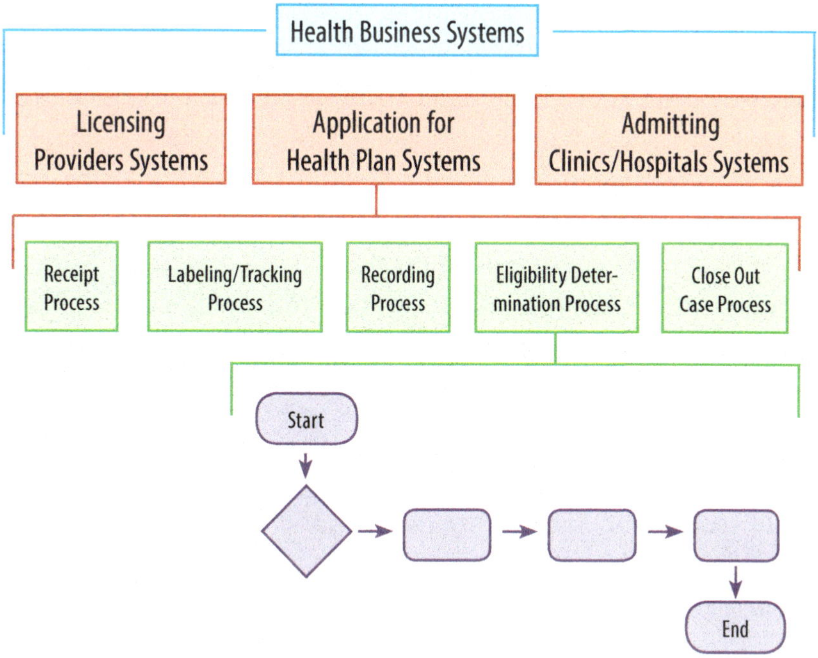

Applications from citizens are submitted for admission to the State Health Plan. (Admission is primarily based on the income of the applicant). The decisions of approval or disapproval take place in a processing center, where the workers' goal is to get the application expedited as quickly as possible and without errors.

The processing center staff is very busy. Many parts of the application are evaluated by the staff for compliance to law. The staff members are also engaged in many other tasks. They communicate with applicants by phone, receive numerous queries as to the status of applications, collect data, store documents, and make decisions by analyzing the applications and validating their information. They complete such tasks by cross-referencing hard copy documents to many external databases. In many instances, their work is interrupted because applications are missing information.

But there is a bigger problem. The processing center is so far behind that they are working on applications today that came into the center 45 days ago. The problem is urgent because applicants have been waiting so long to get their health cards that they have become ill ... and have had to go to the emergency room. This creates a rise in health care costs that is passed on to the taxpayer, something the State Health Plan intended to avoid.

The citizens who submitted applications are frustrated and complaining to their legislators. A decision to launch a rapid process improvement workshop is made, and initial baseline data are collected.

The workshop begins:

1. Workshop Agenda: Understand the current state by reviewing baseline data and observing the process

    a. Review Baseline Data: Volume of Work

Baseline data are needed before improvements can be made and then the same data are collected after improvements are made. They are compared to see the rate of improvement.

The improvement team collected information on the different

kinds of work, and the volume of each. As mentioned earlier, most of the work was:

- Answering phone inquiries
- Processing apps
- Coordinating requests for hearings

The team learned that these kinds of work interacted with one another. For instance, phone calls coming into the center increased as the backlog of processing applications increased. The hearings that were tracked were a result of complaints from clients about their applications being denied. If there wasn't such a backlog, perhaps workers wouldn't hurry and make mistakes. And then requests for hearings would decrease.

b. Review Baseline Data: Time Study

The second set of data was collected weeks before the workshop started. The team needed to know how long it would take one application to get through the processing center from beginning to end. They developed a simple time study. They tracked a sample of 24 new applications. A center staff member received one of the tagged applications and noted the times it came to his/her desk and the time it left his/her desk. This is what the tracking sheet looked like.

Tracking Form for Health Plan Applications Sample

Where is the application? (Note # of application)	When did you get it? Date/Time	When was it done? Date/Time	Your initials, please.

c. Review Baseline Data: Observe the Work Being Done

Nothing is better than seeing the work itself take place. A tour is conducted with the workshop team. They imagined that they are following the piece of paper as it goes through the different work stations.

Work Stations in the Processing Center

- Mailroom Station
- Barcoding Station
- Imaging Station
- Eligibility Station
- Case Closeout Station

The team is instructed to write down the tasks as they are performed and to note where they see delays or bottlenecks.

The tour starts in the mailroom.

They find boxes of mail stacked on the floor and mail in packs tied with rubber bands strewn all over the counters. From the mailroom, they move to the barcoding station. Here the team notes duplication. Some applicants sent their applications through the mail and then also faxed it. This caused a lot of repeat work for the barcoding staff.

Next, the tour goes to the case set-up station. This is where new cases are organized into a file folder, keyed into the data system and folders, and then stored.

© Can Stock Photo

The work team continues its walkthrough to the other stations of imaging, eligibility, documentation, and close-out. With the tour completed, the team has more information about the flow of work.

> "It was interesting for me to follow the application process and imagine it was a person. First, we date-stamp your forehead, put a name tag on you and then throw you in a drawer for 20 days ... " —Sue, team member

2. Workshop Agenda: Analysis

The team gathered so much information, they knew they would not have time to solve all of the problems. They would have to hone in on "where was the most pain?" This was an exercise in separating out the critical few from the trivial many. How did they do this? They looked at the data.

The time study showed that wait time took up 81% of the entire process time. That means that only 19% of the time was the application being worked. The time study broke the data down into the work stations that the application passed through. The data was split into wait time and "being worked on" time. The station with the most pain, that is, the most wait time, was the eligibility station.

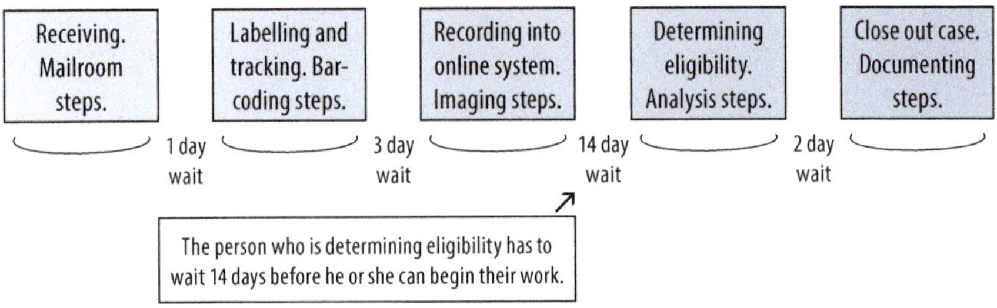

The data showed a 14-day wait before the station picked up an application to start working on it.

3. Workshop Agenda: Improvement recommendations start

Within the eligibility station, there were two major pieces of work going on: validating the application and determining eligibility of the applicant.

This is what the team observed:

- Individual staff members doing the same job were doing it differently. This created variation and added time in the process.
- When staff had to check sources for determining eligibility, they would over-check. That is, when they were checking the third database, they already had the information they needed, but then they went on to check two more databases. This also added time to the process.

The team calculated that the longest period of time was spent on determining the client's income. This step involved going back and forth among different data screens and then cross-referencing between the computer and paper documents ... this all took time.

In the end, the team came up with eight improvement recommendations, most notably one to address the lack of flexibility while moving between multiple screens. All of these improvements went through a "Plan, Do, Study, Act" (PDSA) cycle to test whether the improvement idea would work. Another improvement idea is shown here: removing the mail room altogether.

<table>
<tr><th colspan="3">PDSA Form – MAIL ROOM / BAR CODE</th></tr>
<tr><td colspan="2">Project Team: Rapid Process Improvement</td><td>Report Date: July 17, 2010</td></tr>
<tr><td colspan="3">Improvement Strategy addressed in this cycle:
Eliminate wait time and sorting done in mailroom/bar coding</td></tr>
<tr><td><u>Cycle open/scan make labels</u></td><td>Cycle Begin Date: 06/14/2010</td><td>Cycle Completion Date: 06/14/2010</td></tr>
<tr><td colspan="3">Plan:</td></tr>
<tr><td colspan="3"><u>What</u> we plan to do... (State the basic plan) Fifty applications will be taken from trays as soon as they are received in the mailroom. The person testing, who will be Paul, will run the fifty applications through the "slitting" machine and take to his desk to start the opening and labeling process.
Paul will open each envelope, staple the application and any other documents, date stamp the application and scan any with labels. The applications with no labels will be set aside. Paul will then make the labels for those applications and print the labels and attach to the applications. At this point applications could be immediately assigned to workers.

<u>Who</u> will do this?
Paul

<u>When</u> will it be done?
June 14, 2010 beginning at 7:30 a.m.

<u>Where</u> will this be done?
In the processing center mailroom</td></tr>
</table>

They then prioritized their improvements on a matrix in order to determine the impact of the improvement and how difficult it would be to implement.

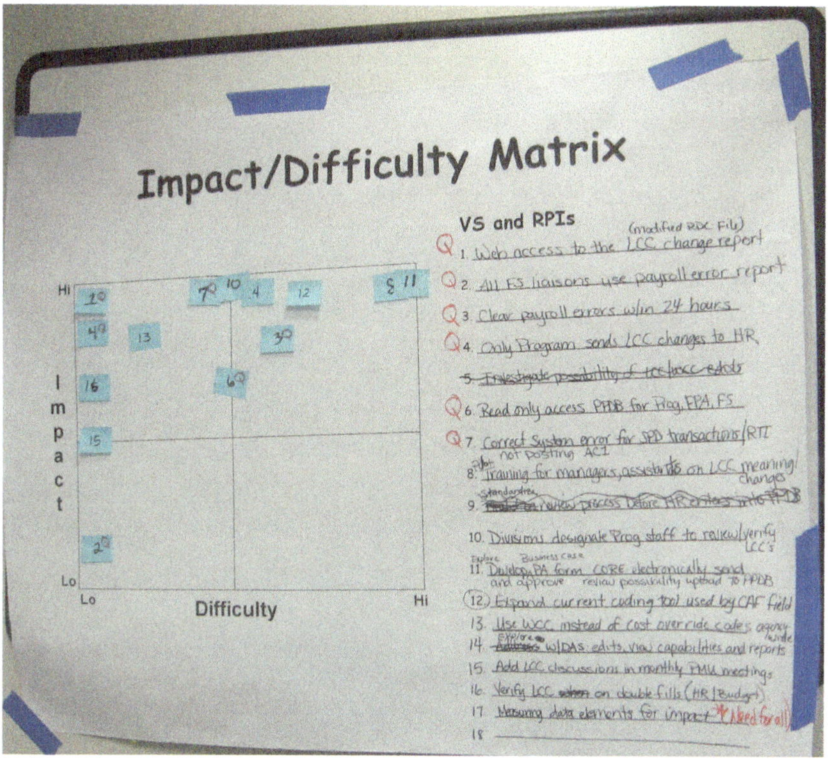

4. Workshop Agenda: Report to management

The workshop prepared and presented the report to the management team. They began by citing the goals of the workshop as stated in the charter. Then they listed the process changes they would recommend to get to a Lean state.

These were the results:

	Baseline	Improvement	Reduction
Processing days	45 days	5 days	88%
Hearings requested	191	131	31%

	Baseline	Improvement	Reduction
Average time to process one eligibility	40 minutes	18 minutes	55%
Overtime hours	869 hours	0 hours	100%

Total savings as a result of the RPI:

Total cost for old process before improvements:	$382, 500
Total cost for improved process:	$121, 200
Money Saved:	$261,300

CHAPTER 3

What must I do before I *invite* Lean into my organization?

It is critical to understand that not every workplace problem is a process problem that can be solved by Lean management. It is much easier to be successful with Lean if you recognize the workplace as being organized into a series of processes. Usually these processes cross departmental boundary lines. This is the biggest paradigm shift for those new to Lean, for Lean requires us to rid ourselves of the silo mentality.

Another thing to do before inviting Lean in is to check your thinking about whether or not you believe you need improving. There are many who have told me that "things are running just fine the way they are; there is no need for improvement." But then I am reminded that there is always change that will affect any organization and change has to be managed. Otherwise, things can get worse, not better. And as referenced earlier, managing change by crisis management is not management at all. It is putting out constant fires where daily heroics get rewarded. This model of management may have worked when nonprofits were smaller and the need was less and dollars were forthcoming, but it doesn't work now.

Asked by the executive director: What I would want to know is where my organization is, in regard to process? And is there a spectrum of improvement levels that I can access along the way to process maturity?

Process maturity, indeed, implies a life cycle to processes. This cycle has different maturity levels and is usually called the Capability Maturity Model, initially used in software development. This is my interpretation of nonprofits' maturity levels of processes:

- Ad hoc (usually used one time)
- Initial (repeatable)
- More developed (documented)
- Mature (processes are measured)

Before you invite Lean into your organization, know what processes you have and their maturity levels. Make a list. Why? Because improvement cannot be made on processes that are short-lived and have only a single purpose. It is understandable that *new* nonprofits have many ad hoc processes, but as the organization grows, some processes, once single-use, begin repeating themselves, becoming more than temporary. Once you have more repeatable, documented, and measured processes, improvement can be applied.

There are different types of improvement that can correspond to the maturity level. The improvement types I use build on each other. That is, you have to have stability with controls before you can move on.

Sequential Improvement Methods

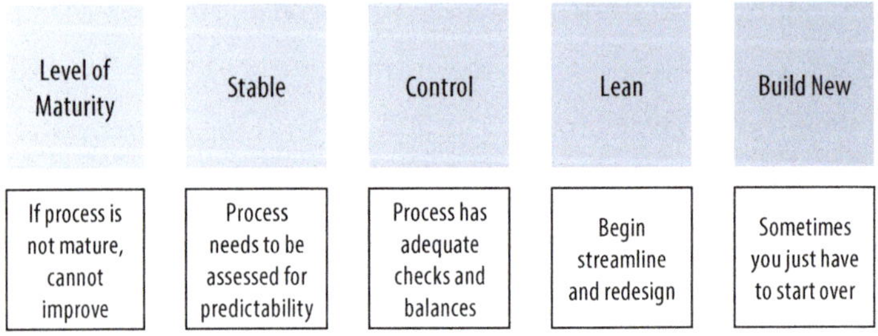

As a former internal auditor, my improvement work always starts with an evaluation of an organization's internal controls. These are the mechanisms in place that prevent fraud and abuse. They are the checks and balances of your financial transactions. There is no use proceeding with any improvement methods until internal controls are in place.

Here is part of an assessment I use to evaluate internal controls:

Internal Controls Self-Assessment

	Never	Rarely	At Times	Usually	Always	Score
20. Documentation – Internal control systems and all transactions and other significant events are clearly documented and the other documentation is available for examination.	0	1	2	3	4	
21. Recording of transactions & events – Transactions & other significant events are properly classified & promptly recorded.	0	1	2	3	4	
22. Execution of transactions and events – Transactions and other significant events authorized and executed only by persons acting within the scope of their authority.	0	1	2	3	4	

As you move from internal controls to the next level of improvements, this is where the streamlining of your processes takes place. *This is Lean work.*

If your organization does not have time to do a workshop, there are shorter sessions that can focus on one part of improvement, such as documenting your processes by flowcharting or finding out the root cause by doing a cause and effect diagram. There are many components of Lean methods that can match your needs.

In the discussion of assessing the maturity of your processes, I said that you needed to list them. Let me elaborate. I was asked to help an IT unit develop an inventory of their processes. Where was I to start? Well, I interviewed each person on the staff and asked everyone what they did. Together we were able to give a name to each process, what each produced, who worked on each, and the name of each process owner. This was an invaluable tool to break down the silo mentality I referred to earlier.

And, last but not least, what you must do to prepare for Lean is embed process thinking throughout the organization. Many do their work so automatically; they are not conscious of their work as a process that as a structure. At the beginning of every improvement workshop, the team is taught how to look at their own work as processes. A dialogue is used by the facilitator to prepare the team for the process work ahead. Here is an example of what you may hear between the facilitator and a team member while the rest of the team is listening:

> Facilitator (F): Please tell the group your job title and the *main thing* that you do in your job. I want you to think about what you do that is repetitive, not just one-time tasks.
>
> Team member (TM): My job title is "provider data entry clerk" and the main thing I do is sit at the computer all day and key in information from filled-out forms.
>
> F: That's great. Let me help you think about this in terms of a process. Remember, I said there was a beginning to a process? The "thing" that begins your work is a form. We call that the input. And I said that something comes out at the end of the process and we call this an output. The output is delivered to the customer.

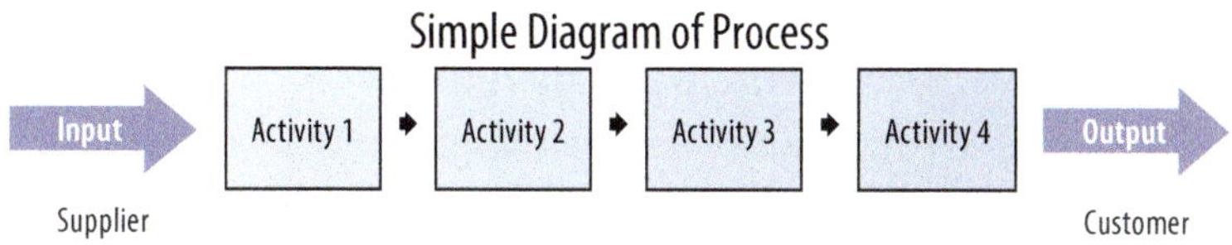

Now let me ask you another question: do you know who your customer is?

TM: We don't have customers!

F: Ah, but you do. The term "customer" is something we are not used to. Think of it as the person who receives your work. For a doctor, the customer would be the patient. For a teacher, it would be a student.

TM: Oh, right. I do the data keying and it comes out on a report that prints off somewhere else and then another person works with that report.

F: Then that person is your customer. That report is the output. That is the "thing" that is produced after you finish all your activities.

TM: You know, I do this every day and sometimes I wonder, is what I do worth it to anyone?

F: That is a great question we should all ask. How does what we do every day fit into the big picture? To help you see how your work aligns with the big picture, let's go through a "so-that chain." Start with the first thing you do in your work and then add "so that" and then move to the next thing you do and add "so that." This is repeated until you reach the end of the process.

TM: I key in data *so that* new healthcare doctors, hospitals, and clinics are registered *so that* they can be paid to provide care to our clients *so that* our clients have access to healthcare treatment. Wow, I do that?

F: And you said you didn't know whether what you did every day was worth it to someone. From your data entry work to a client getting treatment, that is a big contribution.

CHAPTER 4

What does it cost?

One of the costs to adopting Lean involves conducting the initial Rapid Process Improvement workshop and training staff to facilitate future workshops. For the initial workshop, a trained facilitator will have to be hired (if you don't already have one in-house). There is no cost for the team participants because they are your own employees.

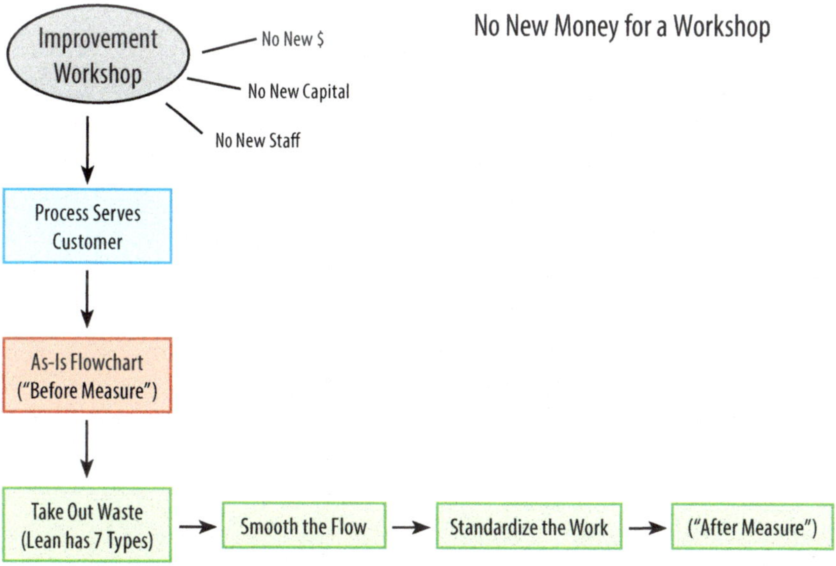

Because of the nature of *kaizen* and how an RPI is set up, there are established parameters for what improvements can be made. Essentially, the improvements have to be feasible to put in place with little or no money. Because of the compressed schedule of an RPI (a few consecutive workdays), recommendations are the kind that can that can be done easily and quickly. There are no long-term, costly projects involved with Lean.

At this point, I would like to pose a different question. "How much does it cost to *not* adopt Lean?"

The Lean literature tells us that most processes have a large percentage of waste in them. "In all the literature I've come across over the years, I see 80 to 95% waste," said Ellen Sieminski, Lean leader at Littelfuse. "I find that hard to believe. In my 12 years of creating value stream maps and helping others create them, that percentage seems to be closer to 98% or 99% most of the time."

We saw this in the case study where the processes included an 81% wait time; that was when the application was sitting idle and not being worked on.

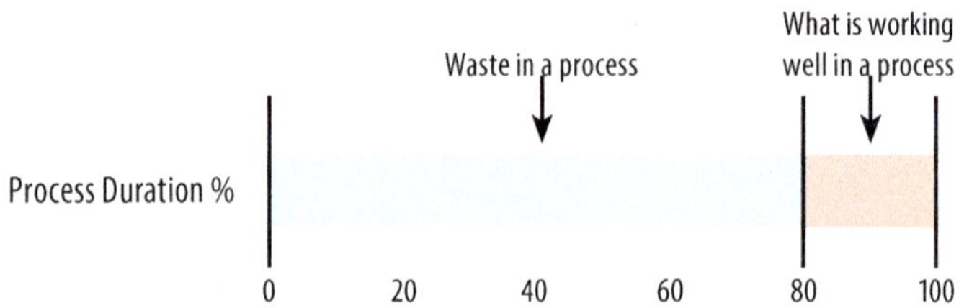

This whole primer is about focusing on reducing that 81% of waste and, by doing this, freeing up more capacity and dollars!

But many organizations do not know about waste and instead are focused on optimizing what is already working well. That would be the 19%. They would throw more money at that 19% to make it better than it already is. Yes, this money would increase customer satisfaction, but not as much as if you rid the organization of waste. Then you would have big increases in customer satisfaction. Imagine the difference in costs!

APPENDICES

APPENDIX A

Where did Lean come from? It has a long legacy.

All new ideas are met with skepticism until they prove themselves. I had the same thoughts about Lean. It wasn't until I learned more about what made up Lean that I realized it had that needed "staying power." I was surprised to learn that Lean is a composite of proven historical management innovations. It has evolved to be called Lean today, but it is part cotton gin, part time and motion studies, and part assembly lines.

Here are just some of the connections I saw:

- **Replacing manual steps with automation** is a Lean characteristic. (In 1799 Eli Whitney invented the cotton gin to automate a long, labor-intensive process.)
- Assuring that work tasks are done in the same way no matter who is doing them is what is called Lean **standardization**. (Frederick Taylor subscribed to work standards in the late 1880s.)
- Utilizing the most **efficient way to organize workflow** is a Lean characteristic. (Henry Ford conceived of the assembly line in auto plants in the early 1900s.)
- The idea that if management understands what "**waste**" is and how it affects a process, they will **learn to reduce it** and thus increase productivity is a Lean characteristic. (W. E. Demings, an engineer, taught this to the Japanese in the 1950s.)

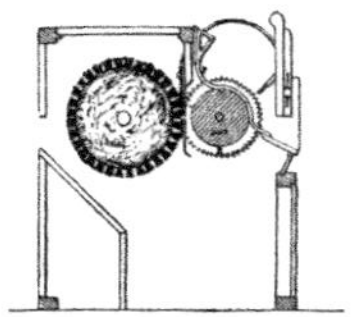

1799—Whitney: invention of the cotton gin automated a long, labor-intensive process

Late 1800s—Taylor: work standards

Early 1900s—Gilbreth: moton study/ process/charting

Ford: Model-T assembly line system

Late 1940s–Early 1950s—Deming, Juran, Iskikawa: reduction of waste, using data to manage processes, quality control

1960s—Ohno: Toyota/ Lean manufacturing

1980s—US adopting Toyota methods, GE develops Six Sigma

2002–2005—Virginia Mason Hospital adapts Lean to hospitals; IRS launches Lean Six Sigma

APPENDIX B

What does a perfect Lean entity look like?

Reading a primer about Lean gives you a glimpse of how it works. Another perspective is how the whole organization works *around* Lean.

NEW SEELAND, Inc.

Let's imagine that the map of New Zealand gives us a shape to portray the infrastructure of an organization that has Lean processes and that values continuous improvement.

You will note that there are two sections, the Strategic Island and the Tactical Island. Goals are set and the objectives to reach them are located on the Strategic Island. The work to carry out the objectives is depicted on the Tactical Island. Both islands are necessary. Communication between the islands is critical, and we imagine a ferry system of information going back and forth.

Let's start where an RPI workshop would take place. It's located in the Tactical Island in the "Can we do better?" Region. Before we have even reached this region, many things have happened to get here. First of all, once the strategies are communicated, processes are developed to implement those strategies. Different measures are used on the processes to see if they are making progress towards implementing the strategies. If they are not, then there is a gap between the planned and the actual. A gap is a problem. If it is a process problem, then the Can we do better? Region resolves the issue, usually with an improvement workshop.

More important than the movement between the islands is the *culture* of this perfectly Lean organization. Lean shows us practices in a work culture to live by:

- A no-blame environment
- Always operating as a learning organization
- Asking the opinions of people who actually do the work
- Last, but not least, a vision of where the organization is going that is communicated to the entire organization

New Seeland is a reference point for you. Wherever you are in a work organization and whatever you do there, know that there are many supports in place for your success.

About the Author

Photo by Kristal Passy Photography

PADDY O'BRIEN has an MPA from Cornell University, a BA from Pitzer College, and is certified in Lean, project management, and communications. She was instrumental in pioneering Lean in many state government services, ranging from child adoptions to motor pools. Her real contribution is sharing "lessons learned" from running over 24 rapid process improvement events. Her recipe for success: stick to the original intent of *kaizen* and believe that front-line workers know the problems best. "With the right tools and guidance, they can solve them." O'Brien has learned from the best consultants, taken all the professional courses, and collected research from multiple Lean databases. She's written this book because, out of all these resources, there are still gaps. She has filled them with her well-thought-out connections between technique, experience in developing workshops, and what historical management innovators have already given us.

Her career, both in the private and public sectors, is a tapestry of different kinds of knowledge and skills. For instance, as a former internal auditor, she brings the importance of internal controls; in organizational development, she brings knowing the stages of team development to facilitation skills. Her experience in collecting data has allowed her to create a list of simple tools easily taught to any worker. And her experience in project management has helped in preparing, facilitating, and closing out an improvement event.

O'Brien has presented at national conferences, been the recipient of multiple awards, and has developed and delivered several courses on Lean, performance measures, and quality tools. She has recently taken leave of full-time state employment to embark on a second career, which includes authoring this book and a coaching manual entitled *Navigating a Rapid Process Improvement Workshop.*

The author can be reached at **obrienlean@gmail.com**.

LEAN for the Nonprofit

What You Don't Know Can Cost You

by Paddy O'Brien

ISBN: 978-1-62901-411-1

Available for purchase on InkwaterBooks.com, Amazon, BarnesandNoble.com, and other popular online bookstores. Also available for order through local bookstores.

CPSIA information can be obtained
at www.ICGtesting.com
Printed in the USA
FSOW04n1520201116
27522FS

9 781629 014111